TO AYLA A...
LOVE AUNT EV...

P.S. DO YOU THINK
THE ENDING OF
THIS BOOK IS SILLY?

HEAD LiCE

For Elie:
May your head be always free of lice

Paperback edition published in 2016 by Tundra Books, a division of Random House of Canada Limited, a Penguin Random House Company

Library and Archives Canada Cataloguing in Publication

Gravel, Elise
[Pou. English]
Head lice / Elise Gravel.

(Disgusting critters)
Translation of: Le pou.
ISBN 978-1-101-91853-1 (paperback)

1. Lice--Juvenile literature. 2. Pediculosis--Juvenile literature. I. Title. II. Title: Pou. English. III. Series: Gravel, Élise. Disgusting critters.

QL540.G7213 2016 j595.7'56 C2015-906950-5

Published simultaneously in the United States of America by Tundra Books of Northern New York, a division of Random House of Canada Limited, a Penguin Random House Company

Library of Congress Control Number: 2014941833

English edition edited by Samantha Swenson
Designed by Elise Gravel and Tundra Books
The artwork in this book was rendered digitally
Printed and bound in China

www.penguinrandomhouse.ca

1 2 3 4 5 6 21 20 19 18 17 16

TUNDRA BOOKS | Penguin Random House

Elise Gravel

HEAD LICE

HEY THERE!

Tundra Books

A single head lice is called

A LOUSE.

Ladies and gentlemen, meet your new louse friend!

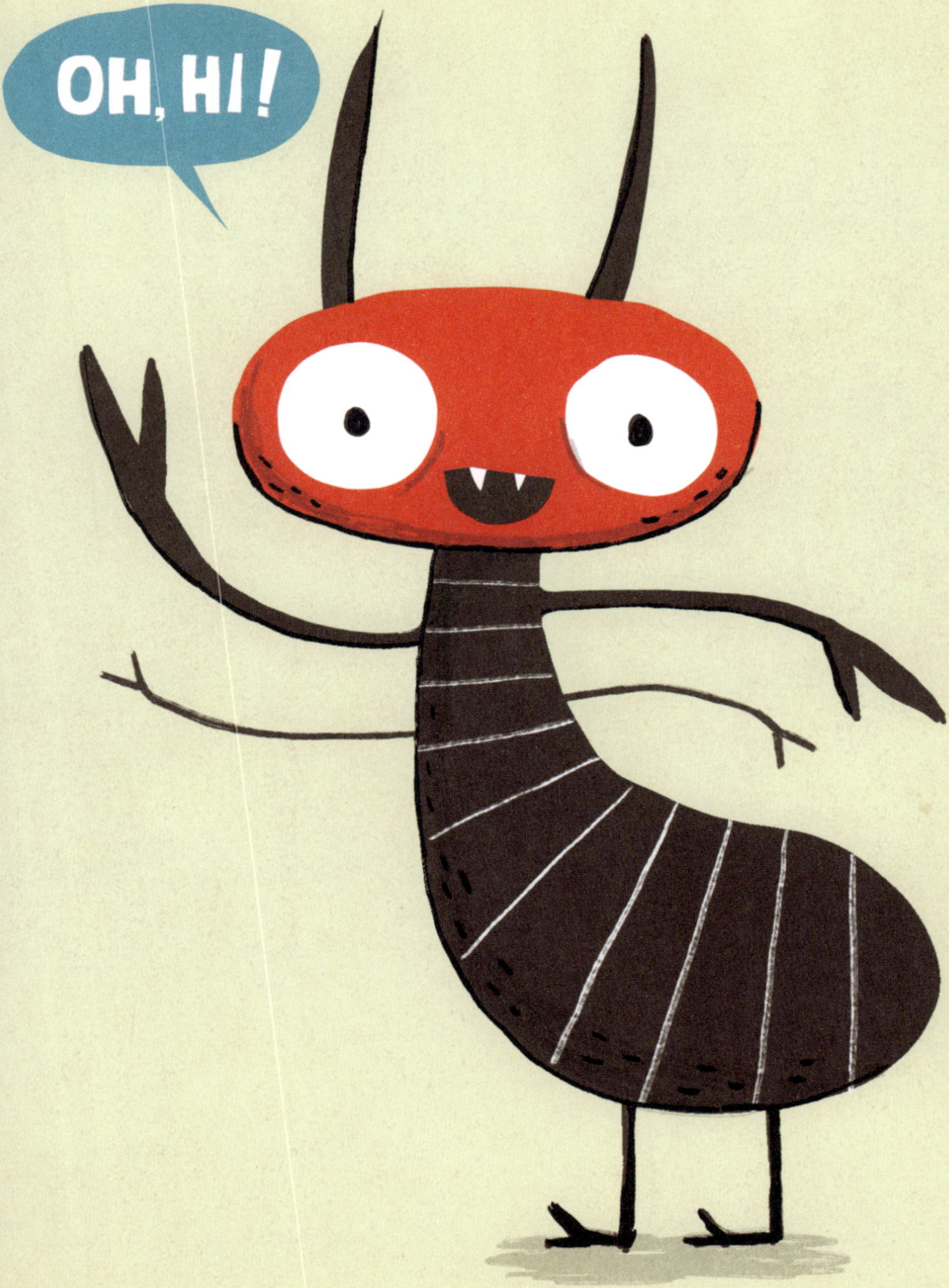
OH, HI!

The head louse has

SIX LEGS,

which makes him an

INSECT.

Well, it's pretty obvious I'm not a FRUIT!

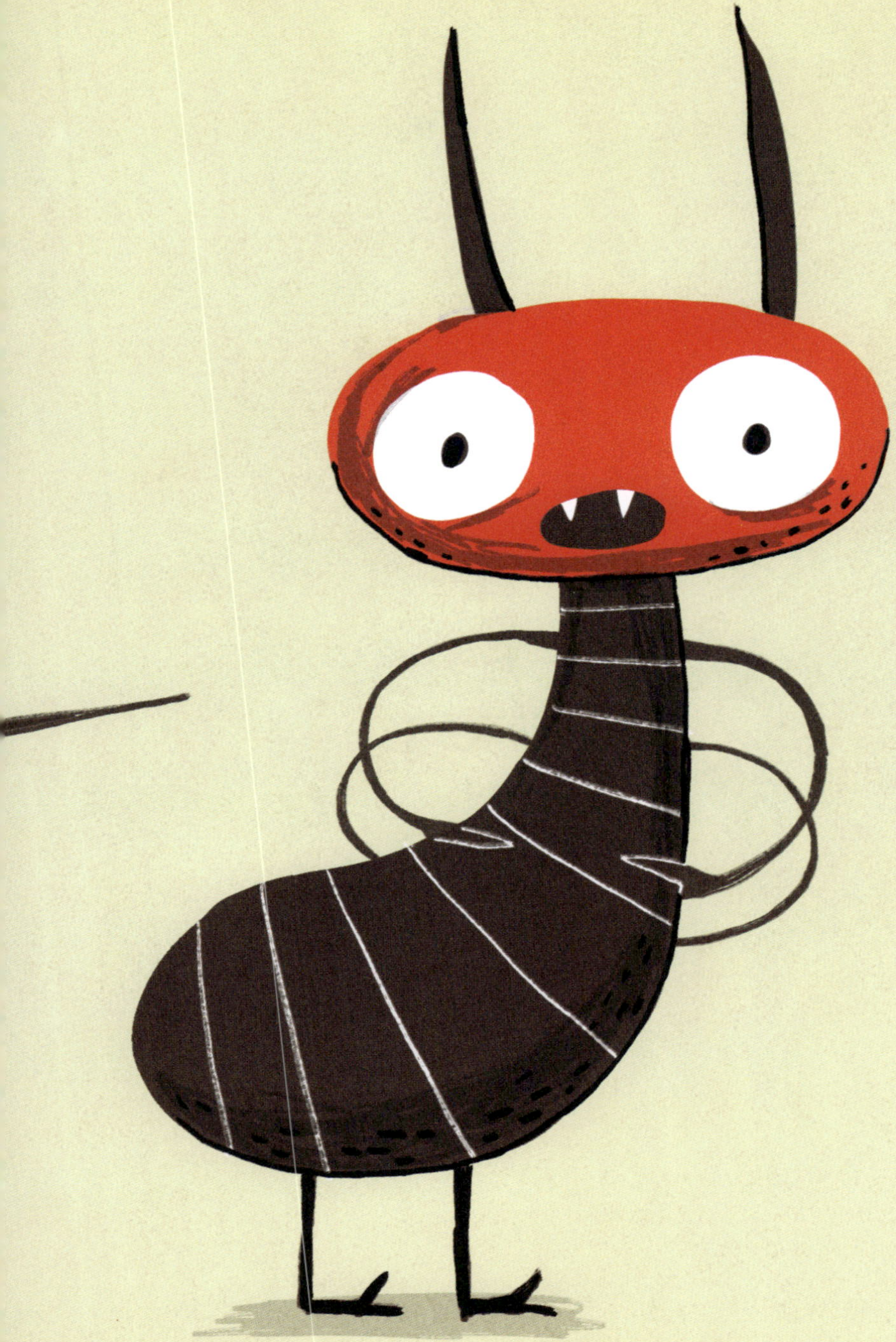

The head louse is about two and a half to three millimeters long, or an eighth of an inch. He's about the size of a

SESAME SEED.

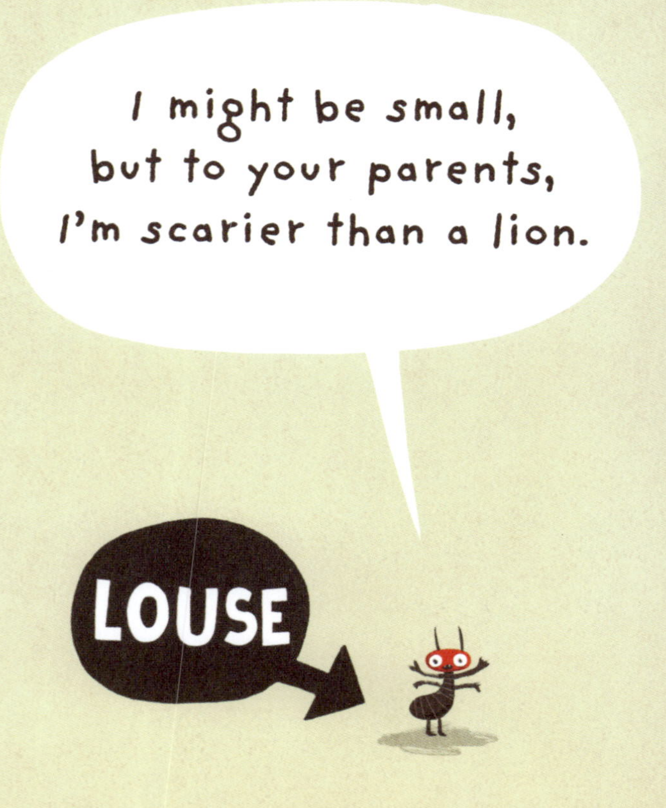

I might be small, but to your parents, I'm scarier than a lion.

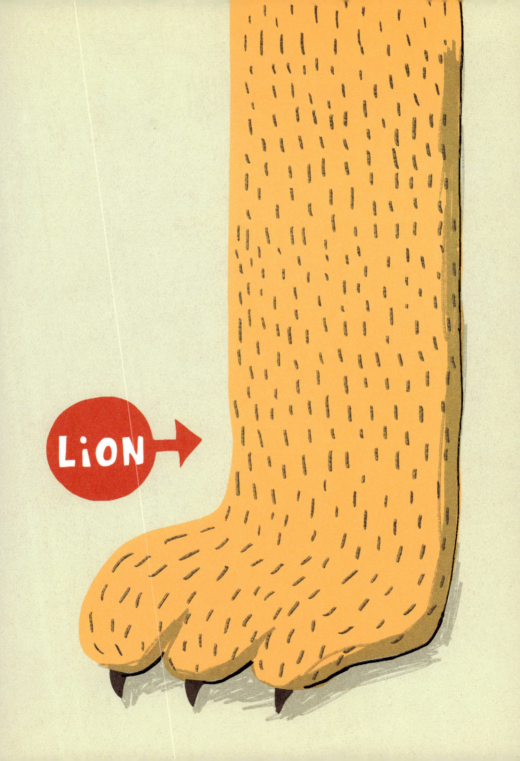

The head louse's body is slightly

TRANSPARENT,

so we can see inside his

TUMMY.

He can't fly or jump, and because of his very

SHORT
LEGS,

he even has trouble walking on flat surfaces.

RRRRRRRRR

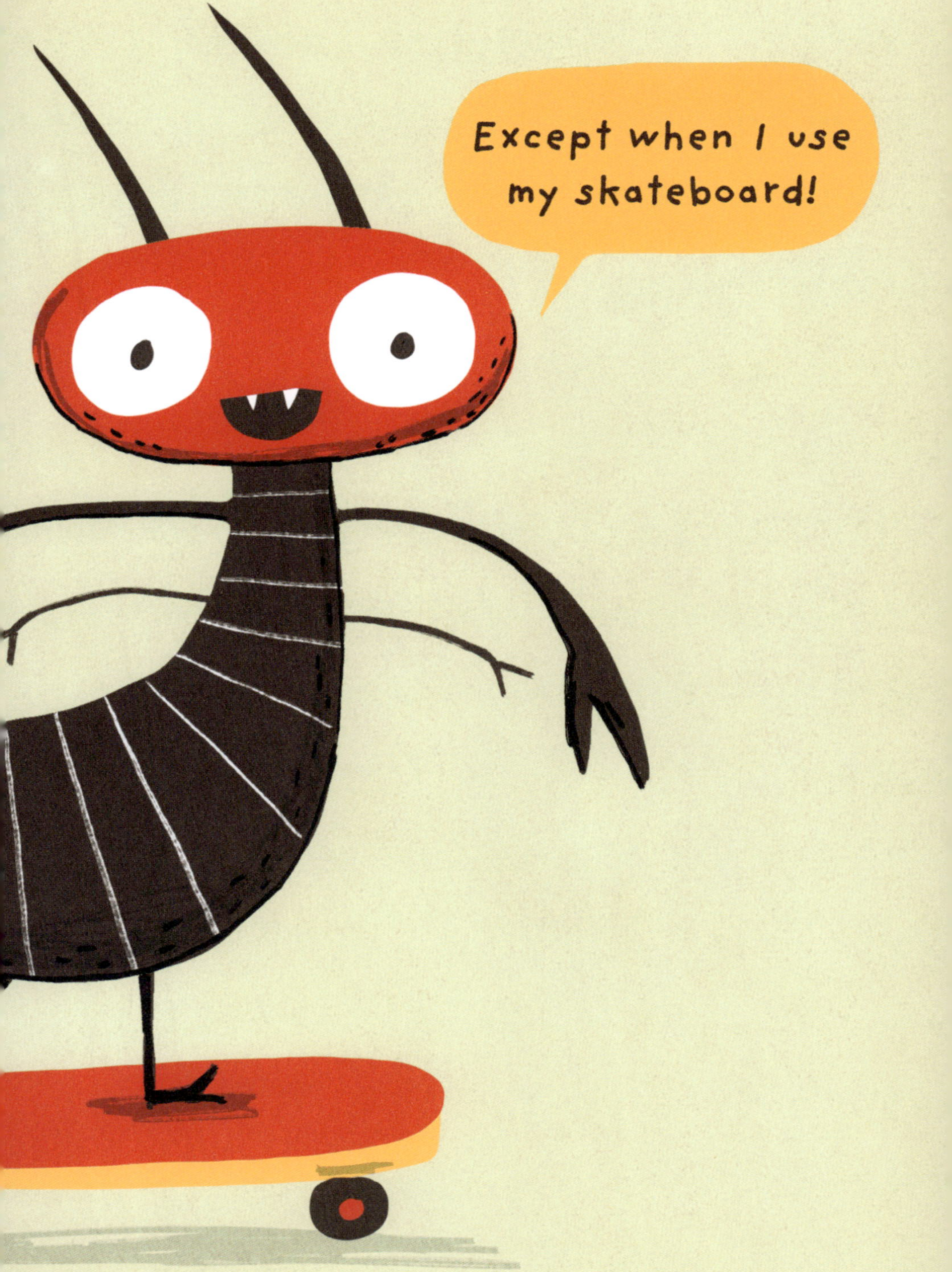
Except when I use my skateboard!

With the use of a big thumb and

CLAW

at the end of his two front legs, he's very good at moving up and down hair and swinging from

ONE HAiR

to another.

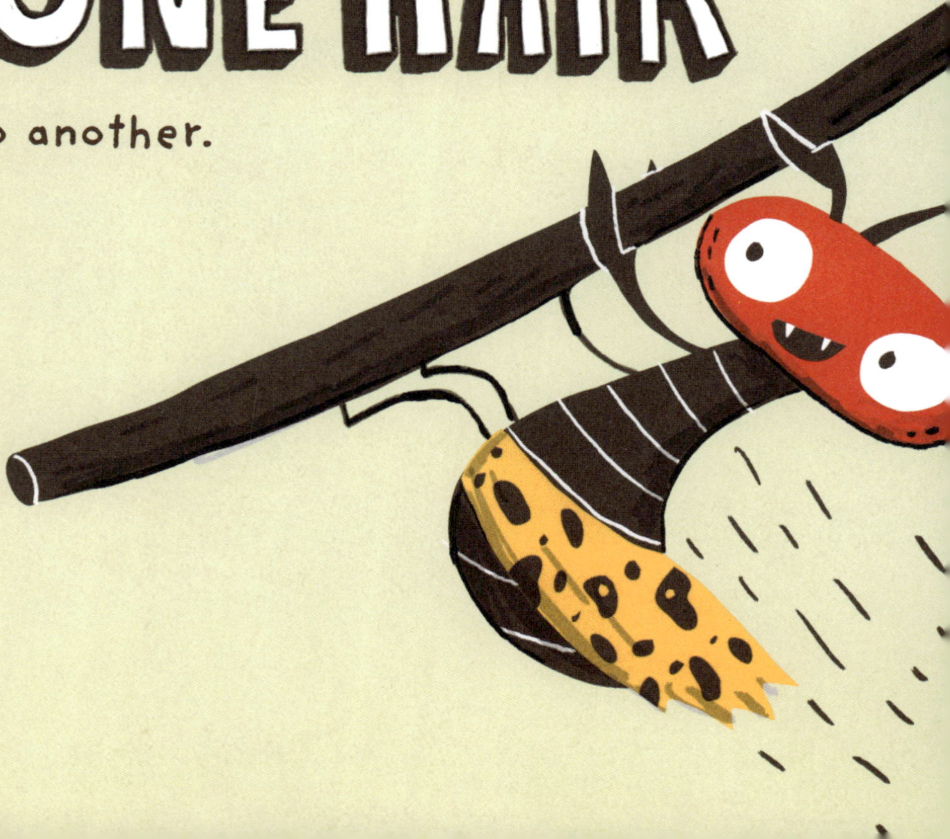

The louse is born, grows up and dies on a

HUMAN

head, and he lives for only 20 to 30 days. He can't live on any other animal or in any other environment.

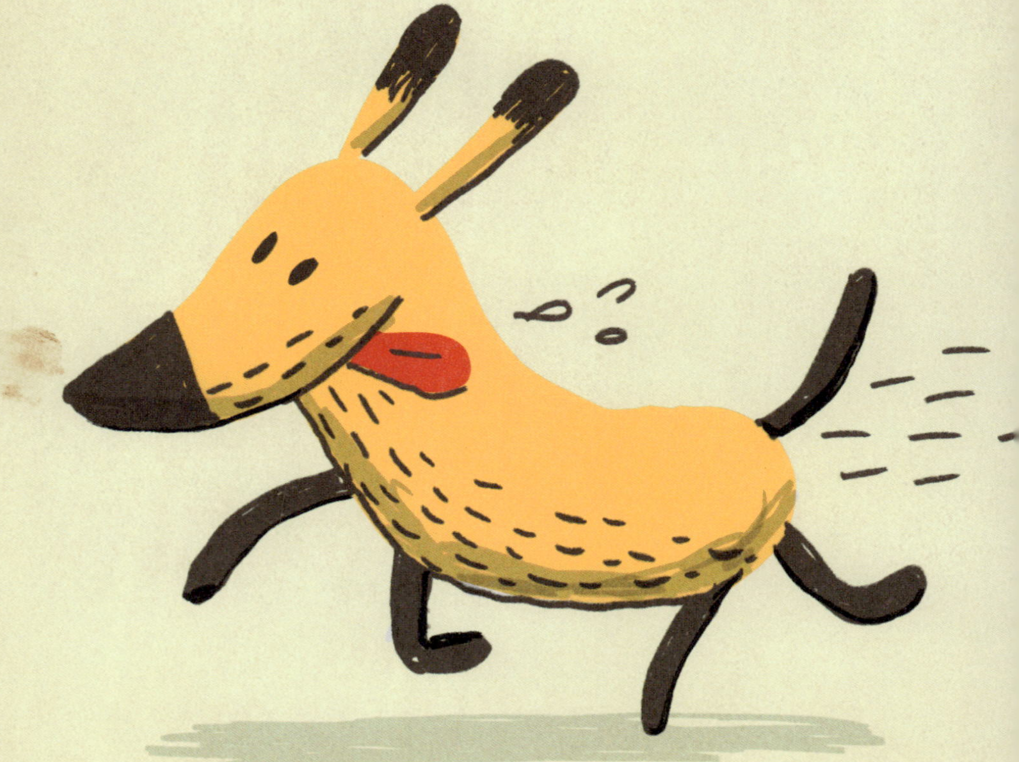

The louse's only food is

HUMAN BLOOD.

He drinks it about five times a day.

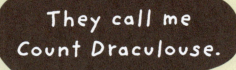

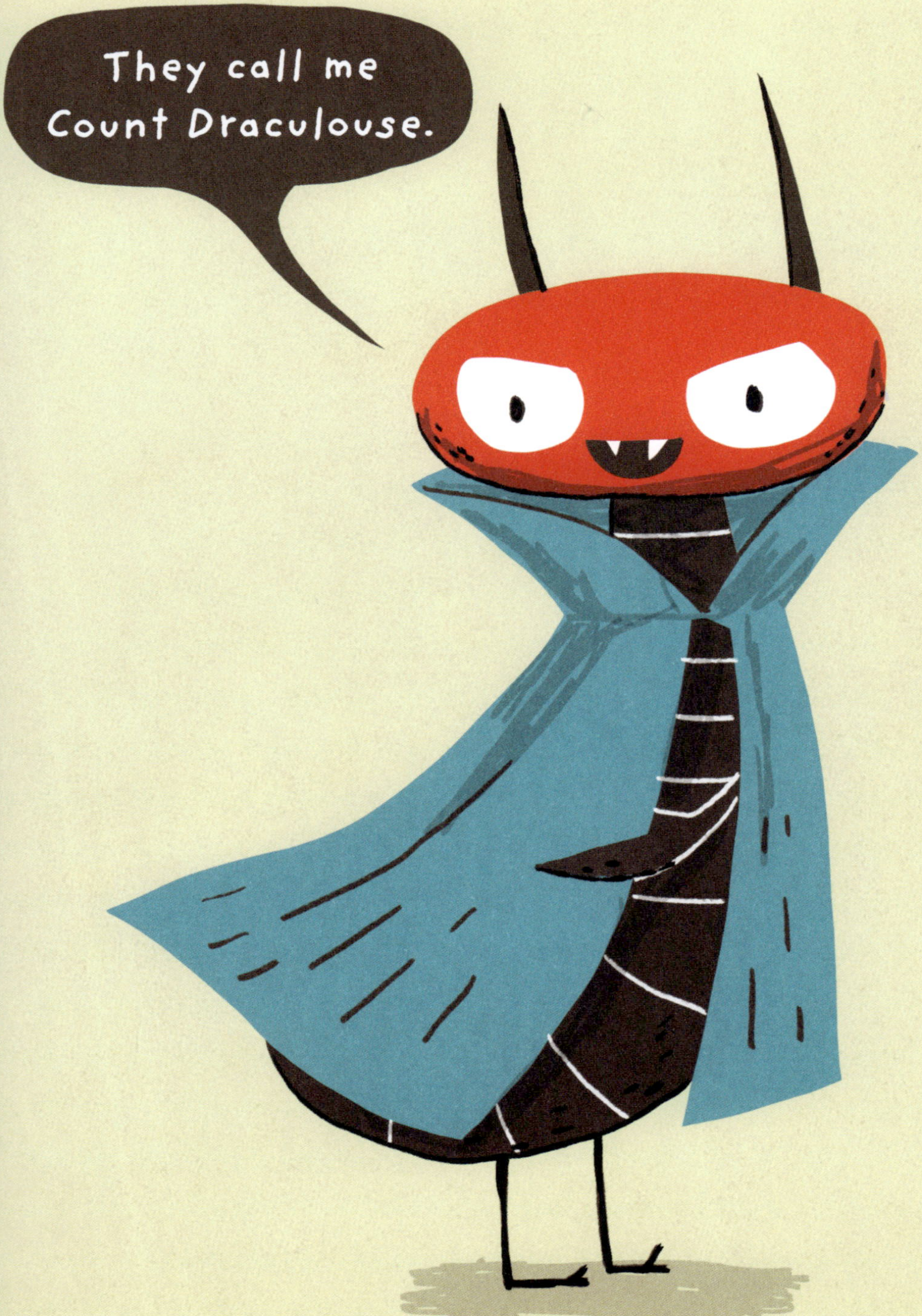

The female louse lays three to five eggs a day. The eggs are called

NITS.

She attaches them to the hair with a very sticky, gluelike substance she makes that hardens like cement.

I also use it to build my model airplanes!

The eggs stay stuck to the hair for seven to twelve days before they hatch. The young head lice, called

NYMPHS,

will soon reproduce too. If you don't get rid of them, you'll end up with a head full of lice!

THEY LIVED HAPPILY EVER AFTER AND HAD MANY, MANY, WAAAAY TOO MANY CHILDREN.

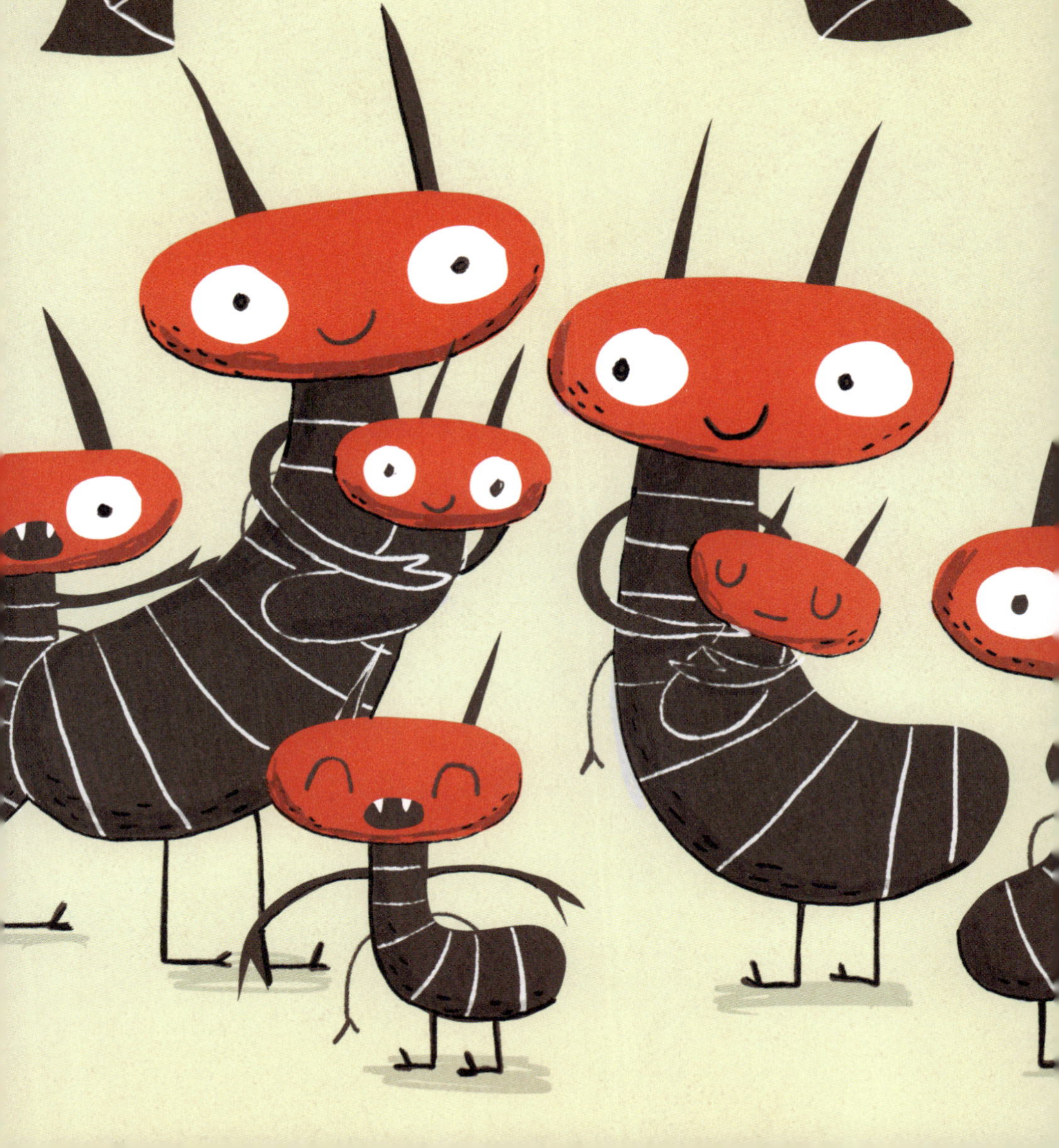

To go from one head to another, the louse has to wait for

HEADS

to touch or for people to exchange hats or clothes with lice on them. He doesn't care one bit if you're clean or dirty!

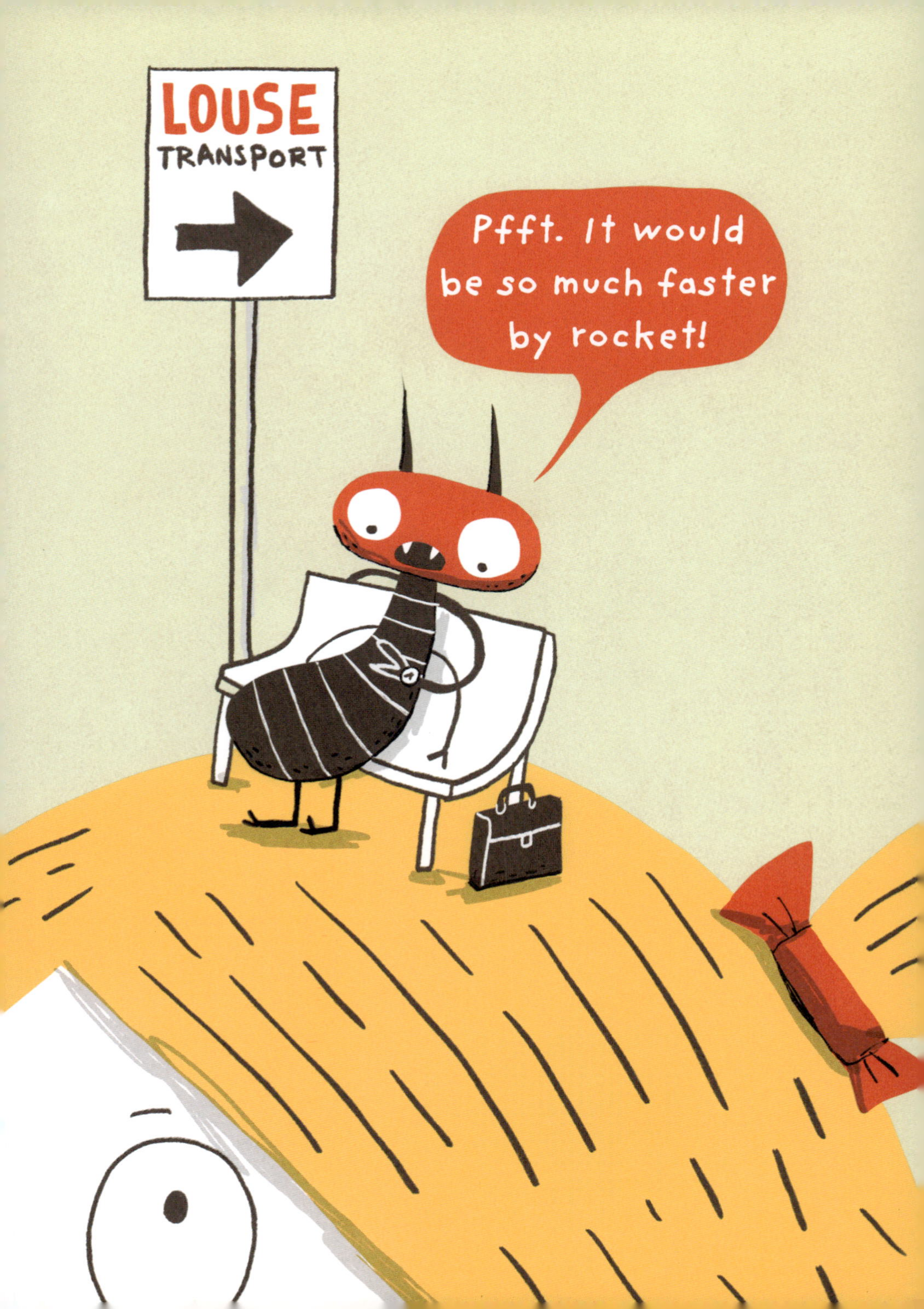

The head louse might be

GROSS AND
ANNOYING

and give you some itchy bites, but he's not dangerous.

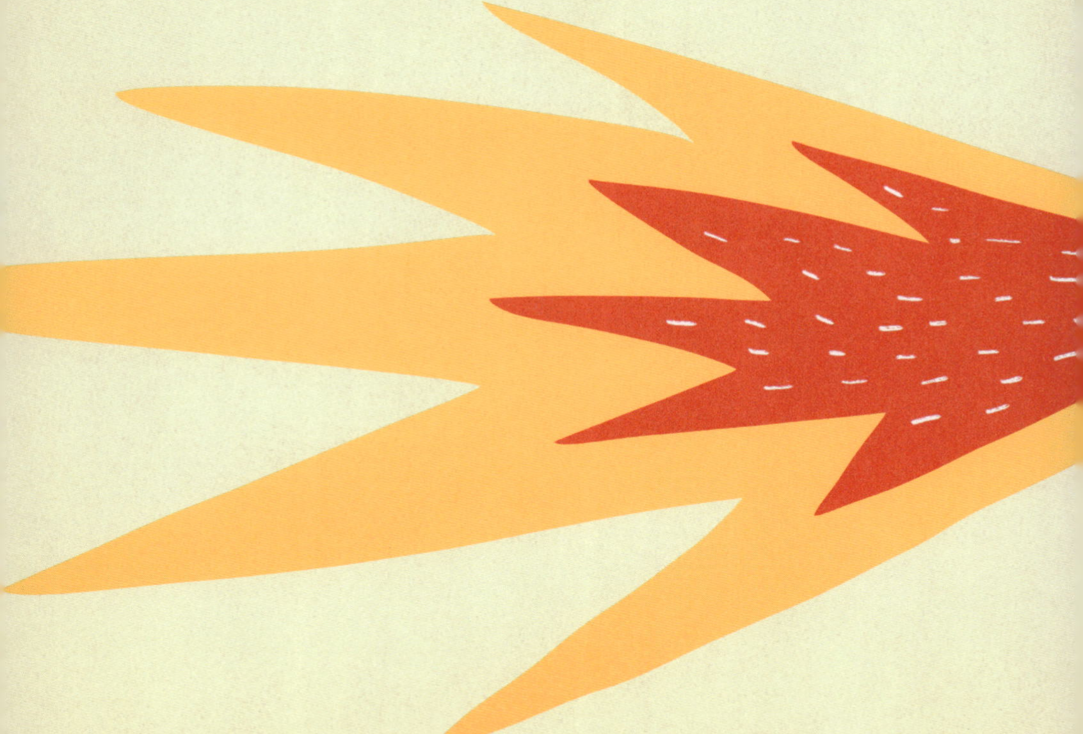

The head louse is really useful for . . .
hmm . . . uh . . . well,

NOTHiNG AT ALL,

really!

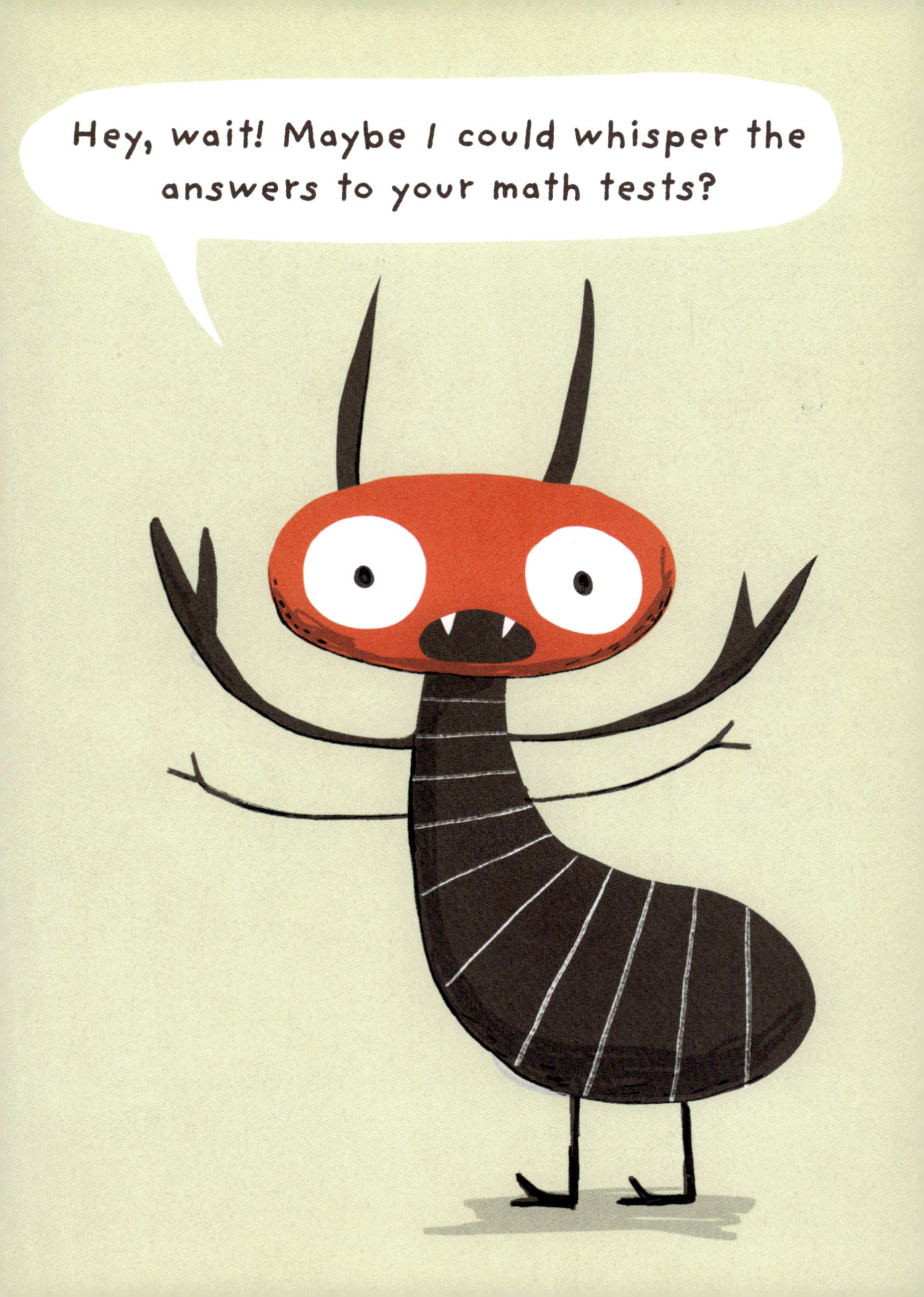
Hey, wait! Maybe I could whisper the answers to your math tests?

So the next time you see a head louse . . .

RUN AWAY!

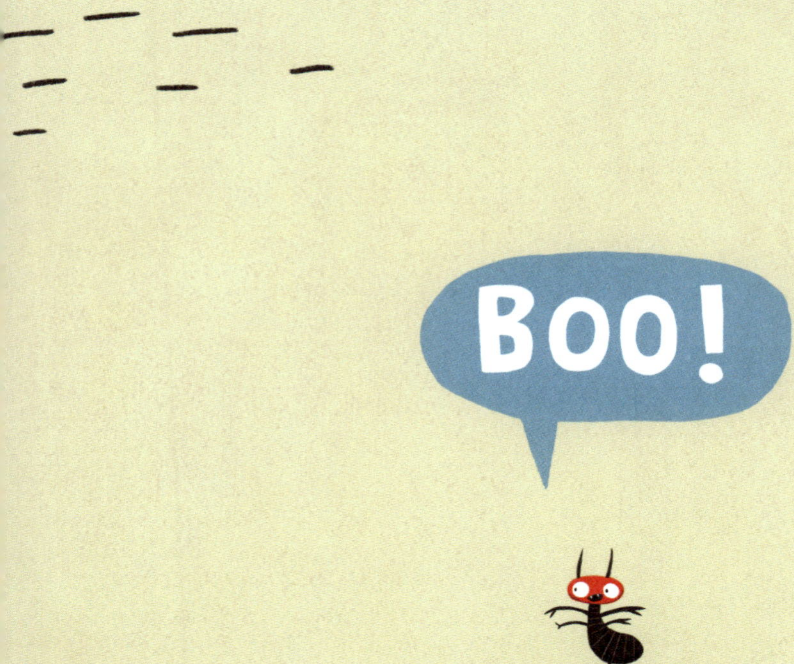
BOO!

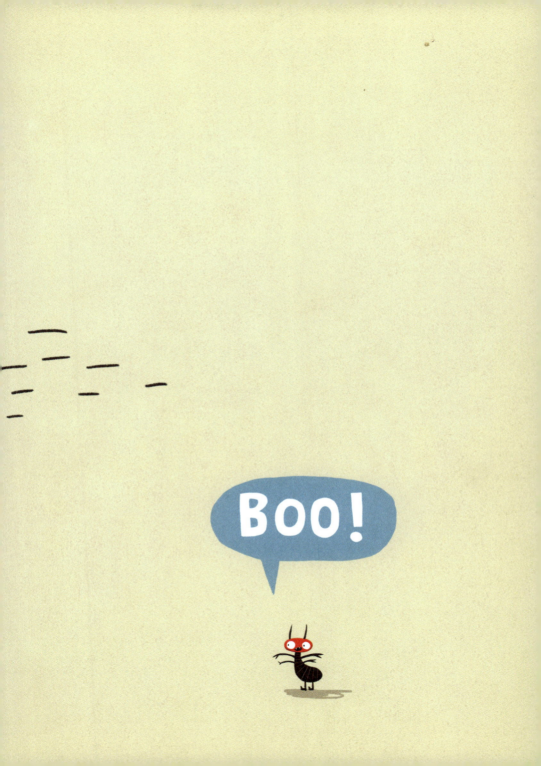

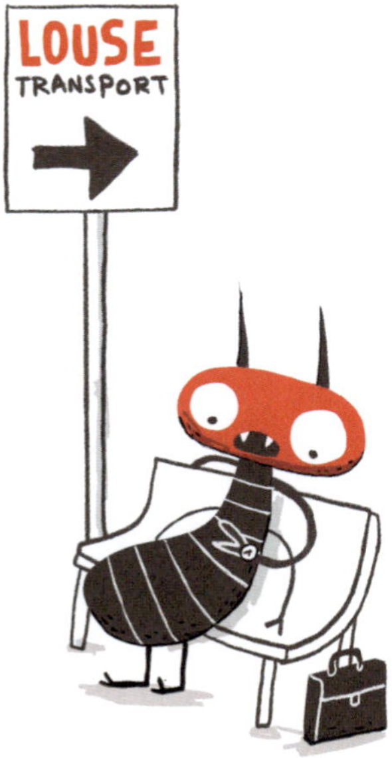
LOUSE
TRANSPORT